DIESELS ON THE EASTERN
Michael Welch and Terry Phillips

Ian Allan PUBLISHING

Front cover: BR/Sulzer Type 2 Bo-Bo No D5070 arrives at King's Cross in July 1965 with a suburban train comprising a rake of Gresley 'Quad-Arts'. Completed between 1958 and 1961, the 1,160hp locomotives later known collectively as Class 24 were constructed at BR's works at Derby, Crewe and Darlington, many being allocated initially to the Eastern Region. This Derby-built example, released to traffic in January 1960 from March shed, would later be renumbered 24 070, ending its career thus in Scotland in February 1976. *Colour-Rail*

Previous page: In years gone by Essendine was a reasonably busy country junction station with branches to Bourne and Stamford in addition, of course, to services on the Great Northern main line. There was a substantial layout with a mechanical signalbox controlling operations at each end of the station. The line to Bourne was closed in June 1951, however, and the short branch to Stamford went the same way on 15 June 1959. Essendine station, which served only a small village, was closed on the same date as the Stamford line. This photograph depicts 'Deltic' No D9001 *St Paddy* speeding past the former station with the down 'Yorkshire Pullman' on 21 July 1962. By this date the down platform had been removed, but the platform, station buildings and goods shed on the up side appear to be intact. *John Beckett*

First published 2008

ISBN (13) 978 0 7110 3264 4

© Michael Welch and Terry Phillips 2008

Published by Ian Allan Publishing

an imprint of Ian Allan Publishing Ltd, Hersham, Surrey KT12 4RG
Printed in England by Ian Allan Printing Ltd, Hersham, Surrey KT12 4RG

Code:0804/B1

Visit the Ian Allan Publishing website at www.ianallanpublishing.com

Introduction

When British Railways was created upon nationalisation on 1 January 1948 it was divided into six regions, one of which was the Eastern (ER). Most of the ER's route mileage had been previously the territory of the London & North Eastern Railway (LNER), the East Coast main line (ECML) south of Doncaster being the most important. The region also served East Anglia, controlling the routes of the erstwhile Great Eastern Railway, and later assumed responsibility for the London, Tilbury & Southend section of the London Midland & Scottish Railway (LMS). The region was significantly enlarged on 1 January 1967 by the addition of the former North Eastern Region but, for the purposes of this album, the ER is defined as that which existed immediately prior to this date.

In 1948 the railway system was predominantly steam-worked, although electric traction was firmly established, particularly on the lines of the former Southern Railway. Diesel traction was very much in its infancy, although the LMS and the Great Western Railway had undertaken some successful pioneering work in developing shunting locomotives and railcars respectively. Significant further progress was, however, delayed by World War 2, and by the early 1950s there were only seven main-line diesel locomotives in service. Of the 'Big Four' companies the LNER had, perhaps, made the least headway and contributed just four shunting locomotives to the BR diesel fleet.

In the first years of nationalisation the ER continued with steam power, taking advantage of the newly built 'Britannia' Pacifics to revolutionise services on the Great Eastern main line to Norwich. However, BR's rapidly worsening financial situation led to the Modernisation Plan of 1955. These proposals, costing £1,200 million, included investment in diesel and electric locomotives, rolling stock, track and signalling. The resulting cleaner, faster and more reliable services would, it was believed, prove more attractive to passengers and freight customers, thus regaining lost traffic. Under the so-called Pilot Scheme various types of diesel locomotive were to be appraised over three years to enable BR to formulate its traction requirements. Eighty of the 174 machines ordered were to be allocated to the ER. However, BR's deficit began to spiral upwards at an increasingly alarming rate and the concept of the Pilot Scheme was scrapped. As a result, large numbers of diesels of inadequately tested design were ordered straight off the drawing board.

The Modernisation Plan also called for significant investment in diesel multiple-unit (DMU) trains, envisaging some 4,600 cars entering service over a three-year period. These units were to be widely used on suburban, rural and inter-city duties and included a number of diesel-electric sets for the Southern Region. Considerable progress had already been made, however, before publication of the Plan. The British United Traction Co had introduced a demonstration train of three four-wheeled cars in 1952. Ultimately 11 cars were constructed, of which seven were powered and four were trailers. They were capable of running as one-, two- or three-car sets and were notable for incorporating a control system that became the basis for that employed in the BR DMU fleet. The cars ran trials on a number of branch lines but were particularly associated with some of the London suburban branches of the London Midland Region. In June 1954 BR implemented its first DMU scheme when eight two-car Derby Lightweight sets went into service in West Yorkshire. Within a few months similar units were introduced on the ER, in Lincolnshire and East Anglia. They proved popular with the public, providing a very much brighter and more pleasant environment than some of the ancient rolling stock they replaced. However, whilst increasing traffic and reducing costs, they ultimately failed to save many rural lines.

The first new main-line diesel locomotive on the Eastern was Type 2 No D5500, one of 20 supplied by Brush Traction Ltd under the Pilot Scheme. This machine was of A1A-A1A wheel arrangement and was powered by a Mirrlees 12-cylinder JVS12T engine developing 1,250hp. Like a number of early BR diesel designs, the Brush Type 2 was rather heavy, weighing no less than 104 tons. Handed over by the manufacturer on 31 October 1957, No D5500 made its first run in passenger service hauling the 10.36am from Liverpool Street to Clacton on 13 November of the same year. The Brush Type 2, the history of which is inextricably linked with the ER, proved successful, and the class eventually numbered 263 locomotives.

The ER, along with the North Eastern and Scottish Regions, also operated what is considered by many enthusiasts to be the most iconic diesel type to run in these islands, the English Electric Type 5 3,300hp Co-Co 'Deltic' locomotive. Developed from a 1955-built prototype, the 22-strong production series ensured that the East Coast expresses remained competitive with road and air transport. Power was provided by two 18-cylinder Napier 'Deltic' engines of 1,650hp. Interestingly the weight of the locomotives was only 99 tons, giving a significantly higher power-to-weight ratio than earlier designs such as the Brush Type 2. Deliveries began in 1961, and the first timetable accelerations were introduced at the start of the 1961/2 winter service. A highlight was the up 'West Riding', which was allowed exactly three hours between Leeds Central and King's Cross, with one stop. Once deliveries had been completed, further improvements were made in the summer 1962 timetable. Three trains in each direction were scheduled between King's Cross and Edinburgh in a level six hours, the best time to Newcastle being a minute over four hours. By the early 1970s track and signalling improvements allowed 'Deltics' hauling eight-coach trains to maintain schedules to Newcastle of 3hr 35min.

Whilst it is not possible in this introduction to highlight all of the diesel classes that operated on the ER at this time, the Brush Type 4 Co-Co deserves mention. For many years these workhorses were responsible for hauling the majority of express services in East Anglia and shared with the 'Deltics' the most demanding services on the ECML. In addition they were frequently to be seen on a wide variety of parcels, mail and freight trains. Fitted with a Sulzer 12LDA28-C 2,750hp power unit, these locomotives were ultimately seen on main routes in virtually all parts of the country, but the first locomotives delivered, commencing in September 1962 with No D1500, were allocated to Finsbury Park depot.

Not all of the locomotives that ran on the ER were a success, however. Both the North British (NBL) Type 1s (Nos D8400-9) and the English Electric Type 2s (the 'Baby Deltics') were unreliable and, consequently, short-lived. For others, such as the British Thomson-Houston Type 1s, which also suffered from poor reliability, changing traffic patterns contributed to an early demise. The NBL Type 2s were, perhaps, the most spectacular failure. These 58 locomotives were originally allocated to the ER but were so unreliable that the complete class was transferred to Scotland in order to facilitate repairs by the Glasgow-based manufacturer. Twenty were re-equipped with Paxman engines from 1964, but those that were not so treated were withdrawn in 1967, after barely eight years' service. The other classes were only a little more fortunate and all (as well as the re-engined NBL Type 2s) had been withdrawn from general service by the end of 1971. Another factor resulting in these classes' early demise was that they were relatively small numerically and, therefore, non-standard, but the financial consequences of such poor investment merely added to BR's financial difficulties.

In compiling this album we have set out to show a representative selection of diesel locomotive and multiple-unit types that worked on the ER during the 20 years or so after the Modernisation Plan was published. We have also tried to illustrate a wide variety of passenger and freight duties. In so doing we have been reminded that, of the many fundamental changes that have occurred on Britain's railway network since 1948, the elimination of the steam locomotive was amongst the first. Thus the photographs feature not only the early diesels (which, in turn, have almost all disappeared) but also many other aspects of railway operation and infrastructure that have largely passed into history. These include attractive country branch lines, gas-lit stations, pre-nationalisation coaches, wooden-bodied four-wheeled wagons, Pullman cars, lower-quadrant semaphore signals and Summer Saturday holiday extras.

We would like to extend our warmest thanks to the photographers who have made their irreplaceable transparencies available for publication. With steam disappearing in 1963 and nothing in the way of spectacular scenery, the ER was little photographed in the period that this book sets out to cover, and we are indeed grateful to those photographers who had the foresight to record what is now as much a part of history as the pre-nationalisation period. We would also like to thank our wives, Theresa and Christine, for their endless support and patience during the preparation of this book

Terry Phillips
Fareham, Hampshire

Michael Welch
Burgess Hill, West Sussex

Left: A view inside the echoing vault of King's Cross station on 25 August 1976 shows Class 47 No 47 546 arriving at Platform 8 at the head of the 'Yorkshire Pullman', which included through coaches from Harrogate. At this time expresses on the East Coast main line were still largely the preserve of Class 47s and 'Deltics', the first High Speed Train workings not being introduced until May 1978. No 47 546 was ordered in September 1962 and entered service in July 1964 as D1747. It was renumbered 47 546 under the TOPS scheme in 1974 and would later be named *Aviemore Castle*, in a ceremony at Aviemore station on 8 May 1985. Condemned in January 2000, it was broken up at Wigan four months later. *Hugh Ballantyne*

Above: In this April 1966 picture a DMU train, formed of a pair of two-car units, is depicted bouncing out of King's Cross, apparently (if the rear destination blind is to be believed) heading for Cambridge. Part of the station's former signalbox, which was such a towering landmark, can be seen on the right of the shot. Vehicle No E56430 was a Driving Trailer Composite Lavatory (DTCL), built by Cravens of Sheffield and released to traffic in September 1958. It weighed 24 tons and provided 12 first- and 51 second-class seats. Many of these sets were delivered to Lincoln and Cambridge depots when new but were soon moved to Hornsey to take over suburban workings on the Great Northern line from King's Cross. This particular car survived until September 1978 and was broken up by Kings of Snailwell, near Newmarket, in June 1980. *Colour-Rail*

Left: By 1965 the steam era at King's Cross was over, and the powerful (3,300hp) 'Deltic' Co-Co diesel locomotives were the most impressive engines regularly seen at the terminus. They were equipped with two Napier 'Deltic' 1,650hp engines that powered six axle-hung, nose-suspended traction motors. These locomotives, which were booked for the most demanding ECML duties, weighed 99 tons and had 3ft 7in driving wheels. In this portrait from August 1965 train tail-lamps and barrows litter the platforms as No D9012 *Crepello* erupts into life at the head of the 6.05pm King's Cross–Newcastle, which train was rather unimaginatively named 'The North Eastern'. On the right, almost lost in the shadows, is an unidentified 'Baby Deltic', whilst just creeping into the picture on the left is Brush Type 2 No D5625, presumably with a train of empty coaching stock. *David Mitchell*

Left: The exhaust fumes from *Crepello* (and, apparently, those from another departing train) come close to obscuring Gasworks Tunnel in the background as it departs with the train seen in the previous shot. No D9012 entered service on 4 September 1961 and was one of eight of the class named after racehorses, the nameplates being fitted at Doncaster Works without ceremony prior to its entering traffic. It was initially allocated to Finsbury Park depot and had its moment of glory on 18 June 1962 when it powered the inaugural diesel-hauled 'Elizabethan' express from King's Cross to Edinburgh. In October 1979 white window surrounds were applied by Finsbury Park, a depot well known for its local embellishments. *Crepello* remained in service until 18 May 1981 and was broken up three months later. *David Mitchell*

A fuelling/stabling point was provided at King's Cross to facilitate the quick turnaround of locomotives off incoming trains and obviate the need for them to go to Finsbury Park depot for fuelling purposes. In this picture, which was taken on 28 September 1966, a number of locomotives cluster around this facility, the most prominent being English Electric 2,000hp Type 4 (later Class 40) 1Co-Co1 No D256. Brush Type 4 (later Class 47) No D1529 and a Brush Type 2 (later Class 31) add to the variety. On the extreme right can be seen another Brush Type 4, apparently entering Gasworks Tunnel. Note the extremely complicated track layout on this side of the station throat, which incorporated two three-way points; doubtless there were more outside camera range.
Terry Phillips

A further view of King's Cross on 28 September 1966 shows 3,300hp 'Deltic' No D9013 *The Black Watch* coming off the fuelling point prior to powering the 12.00 King's Cross–Aberdeen. The train-reporting number visible in the picture indicates that No D9013 had arrived in the capital some hours earlier at the head of the 'Aberdonian', the 20.30 Aberdeen-King's Cross sleeping-car train. No D9013 entered traffic at Haymarket shed, Edinburgh, on 14 September 1961 and ran nameless for over a year, finally being named on 16 January 1963 in a ceremony at Dundee. It lost its appealing green livery during an overhaul at Doncaster Works in December 1967, emerging in ghastly (in the opinion of many rail fans) corporate blue with full yellow ends. In the mid-1970s a number of 'Deltics' received a 'heavy general repair', which was particularly extensive and included renewal of the inner/outer body skins and complete electrical rewiring. By that time their replacement on the fastest ECML expresses by HSTs was on the horizon and, in view of the expenditure involved in this work, only four locomotives were so treated. No D9013 was the last to undergo this overhaul but did not receive the 'full treatment' due to cost considerations. *Terry Phillips*

Above: Having just emerged from the tunnel, empty stock from a morning commuter service to Moorgate passes the suburban station's terminal platforms on 23 April 1974 behind Class 31/1 No 31 224. Visible above the train is the roof of St Pancras station. *Chris Evans*

Left: A Cravens-built four-coach DMU waits at King's Cross (York Road) platform as passengers disembark. This picture was taken on 16 October 1976, at which time certain rush-hour trains from outer-suburban stations continued from here to Moorgate, in the heart of the City of London.
This extremely useful connection originally came into use on 1 October 1863, but by the date of this picture its days were very much numbered, as it was about to be superseded by a new direct link from Finsbury Park to Moorgate via Drayton Park. Official closure of the King's Cross–Moorgate line came on 8 November 1976, although the York Road platform remained in use for terminating trains only until the spring of 1977. It should be pointed out that this was the up line to Moorgate; the down connection was via Hotel Curve, on the other side of King's Cross main-line station and served by a platform in the suburban station. *David Mitchell*

The first 12 miles or so out of King's Cross are graded against northbound trains and in steam days must have presented quite a challenge to footplate crews in charge of a 'cold' engine. The first mile from the terminus rises at 1 in 107, but even this is unlikely to have troubled the crew of 2,750hp Brush Type 4 Co-Co No 1104 as it takes the 10.15 express to Newcastle upon Tyne past Belle Isle on 1 September 1973. This was a dated train that ran only at the height of the summer; hence it is composed of Mk 1 stock. This locomotive was one of 12 of these machines numbered in a separate series (D1100-11) when all of the available numbers in the main series (D1500-1999) had been allocated. Constructed at Crewe, it entered service on 19 October 1966 and subsequently became No 47 521 under the TOPS scheme in March 1974. It was broken up by contractors, coincidentally also at Crewe, in July 1995. *Chris Evans*

English Electric 'Deltic' Type 5 No D9017 *The Durham Light Infantry* roars past Holloway South Down signalbox with the 'Harrogate Sunday Pullman' the 9.40am King's Cross–Harrogate, on 4 October 1964. Note the vintage Pullman brake vehicle immediately behind the locomotive, while the remainder of the carriages visible are more modern Metro-Cammell Pullman coaches, fitted with Commonwealth bogies, which were introduced in the early 1960s. The 1928-built Pullman brake vehicles continued in service until replaced in 1965/6 by BR Standard Mk 1 Full Brake (BG) coaches. No D9017 entered traffic in November 1961 at Gateshead depot and survived until January 1983, when it was cut up at Doncaster Works. *Hugh Ballantyne*

Left: The 12.30 Baldock–King's Cross train approaches Finsbury Park station on 2 April 1974. Twenty of these three-car suburban units were built at Derby Works in 1958/9 and were originally employed on Lea Valley services, their high power-to-weight ratio enabling them to keep pace with the EMUs that shared the tracks into and out of Liverpool Street station. When the Lea Valley line was electrified the units were transferred to the Great Northern section, where they worked London-area suburban services alongside Cravens (later Class 105) units. The Derby units had the unique 'orange star' coupling code because of their hydraulic transmission and straight pneumatic controls, rather than the electro-pneumatic system used on most other ('blue square') DMUs, and the fact that the two types could not work in multiple no doubt caused some operational problems. All of these Class 125 units, as they had become, would be withdrawn as non-standard in 1977. *Chris Evans*

Left: Wood Green station (later renamed Alexandra Palace) is the location of this picture, taken on 6 July 1974. Judging by the shed (on the right-hand side), partly demolished footbridge and temporary lighting, the premises were undergoing modernisation; or was it, perhaps, 'rationalisation'? The train is the 17.18 King's Cross–Cleethorpes, formed of a uniform rake of Mk 2 passenger coaches with a Mk 1 brake van (BG) immediately behind travel-stained Class 47 Co-Co No 47 223. Almost 10 years after the introduction of corporate blue livery locomotives could, as here, still be seen in green. *Chris Evans*

Above: Nice locomotive, shame about the coaches! Commuters on the Great Northern line doubtless wholeheartedly welcomed BR's plans to modernise the line but would probably have preferred it to have started with improvements to coaching stock rather than new motive power! Brush Type 2 A1A-A1A No D5679, hauling a down train at Hadley Wood on 9 May 1963, looks impressive enough and, indeed, was a mere two years old at the time of this photograph, but the carriages, in sharp contrast, are two ancient wooden-bodied 'Quad-Art' sets that dated from the 1920s and were extremely cramped and uncomfortable. The people with the most spacious accommodation on this train would undoubtedly have been the driver and guard! The 'Quad-Art' stock was later replaced by BR Standard non-corridor suburban stock, which was almost luxurious by comparison. *Roy Hobbs*

Right: An imaginative picture of the down 'Yorkshire Pullman' entering Hadley Wood Tunnel behind 'Deltic' No D9007 *Pinza* on 8 June 1963. In addition to serving the principal cities of Leeds and Bradford this service included through carriages to Hull and Harrogate. No D9007 entered traffic in June 1961 at Finsbury Park depot and would be renumbered under the TOPS scheme in February 1974. Withdrawn in December 1981, it was cut up eight months later at Doncaster Works. *John Beckett*

The passenger timetables of the early 1970s still included a dwindling number of summer-dated extra trains, especially on Saturdays, which was still the traditional day on which holidays began and ended. On the Great Northern main line one of the most interesting workings was the 13.35 Skegness–King's Cross, which regularly produced a pair of Brush Class 31s, a single locomotive being deemed unable to run sufficiently fast to keep clear of the 'Deltics' on the double-track sections. Even at Welwyn North, just 22 miles from King's Cross, there were only two tracks because of the enormous expense of quadrupling across the lengthy Welwyn Viaduct as well as boring further tunnels. Nos 31 108 and 31 207 are seen passing the picturesque station with the up service from Skegness on 6 July 1974. Note that the train appears to be made up of a 'scratch' rake of coaches; whilst some are clean, others appear to be in dire need of a trip through the carriage-washing machine. *Chris Evans*

One of the most contentious and bitterly fought closures during the era of Beeching cuts was that of the useful cross-country Oxford–Cambridge line. In the event, the Government of the day saw fit to reprieve only the Bletchley–Bedford section, which remained open for passengers. Other stretches of the line stayed open for freight, but the Bedford–Cambridge section was closed completely. The last day for passenger trains on this stretch of line was 31 December 1967, on which date a Derby 'Lightweight' DMU is seen arriving at Sandy on a service to Oxford. The tracks in the background are those of the East Coast main line. *John Beckett*

Left: A down Civil Engineer's Department working is seen near Offord, south of Huntingdon, on 21 July 1962 with 'Baby Deltic' No D5901 in charge. This class, which was introduced in 1959, could hardly be described as a glittering success, and by 1963 all were dumped out of use at Stratford because of their chronic unreliability. They were later rebuilt, and some improvement was achieved but in the late 1960s BR formulated a National Traction Plan in which small, non-standard locomotive classes found little favour. Most of the 'Baby Deltics' were withdrawn in 1968/9, but two examples soldiered on until 1971. No D5901 was destined to survive the longest of all, being commandeered by the Railway Technical Centre in 1969. It was finally withdrawn from departmental use in November 1975 and later scrapped at Doncaster.
John Beckett

Left: Bound for London on a sunny 13 February 1971, an unidentified Class 47 passes Peterborough at the head of the 'Yorkshire Pullman'. This was the last working on the East Coast main line to include second-class Pullman vehicles, some of which, in umber and cream, can be seen in the formation. Unlike the first-class cars they were never repainted in grey/blue livery and were withdrawn from 3 May 1971, some subsequently eking out an existence in East Anglia as First Open (FO) coaches, whilst others worked in Motorail sets and on excursion trains. Note the tiny signalbox, which presumably controlled movements at the north end of the station; also the remarkable array of semaphore signals of various shapes and sizes.
Terry Phillips

Another view of the north end of Peterborough station, taken more than three years later, on 3 July 1974. Spot the differences! By this date the signalbox and semaphore signals had been swept away as part of a modernisation scheme that involved revising the track layout to permit faster running and the building of an additional platform, which can be seen on the right. The train in view is the 'Hull Pullman' with Class 47/4 No 47 409 in charge, hauling a formation that includes Mk 2 air-conditioned coaches, Mk 1 catering vehicles and three Pullman cars (on the rear). On the left can be seen Class 40 No 40 070; also visible are an unidentified Class 45 and a Class 25. *Hugh Ballantyne*

A Toton–Whitemoor coal train, hauled by green-liveried BR/Sulzer 2,300hp 'Peak' No D1 *Scafell Pike,* approaches Peterborough during the afternoon of 13 February 1971. No D1 was the first of 10 such machines built at Derby Works in the late 1950s and entered traffic in April 1959. All 10 were based at Camden shed, being used initially on Euston–Manchester trains and other West Coast duties; however, they were quickly relegated from top-link work and spent most of their careers based at Toton for working coal trains, principally to Whitemoor, as seen here. Despite the unexciting nature of these workings this distinctive class gained celebrity status, especially when BR dropped the 'D' prefix to locomotive numbers and nine of them were reduced to a single digit on their bodysides! *Scafell Pike* was among the first casualties, being condemned in October 1976, but other representatives lasted considerably longer, the last being withdrawn in late 1980. Such was the popularity of these locomotives that two were bought for private preservation. *Terry Phillips*

Right: BR green livery suited the English Electric Type 4 1Co-Co1 locomotives well, and in this portrait No D355 makes a fine sight near Corby Glen with the 3.45pm King's Cross–York express on 21 July 1962. This particular machine was one of the later batch (Nos D345-99), with a centrally placed headcode display panel. The train is formed principally of BR Standard Mk 1 vehicles, the exceptions being the first and third coaches, which are Thompson- and Gresley-designed respectively, the former easily recognisable by its white oval lavatory windows. *John Beckett*

Right: The English Electric Type 4s were versatile locomotives and were equally at home on passenger and goods trains. Indeed, many of the class spent their declining years in the north of England working heavy coal trains across the Pennines, but in the summer months they were quickly promoted to working seasonal extras on an 'out and home' basis that sometimes involved quite long distances. In this picture, also taken on 21 July 1962, an unidentified member of the class is seen near Corby Glen with a down goods. Included in the consist are short-wheelbase wagons that were restricted to 45mph due to their lack of stability at high speed, so it is unlikely the train was moving very quickly when it passed the photographer. *John Beckett*

The up 'Anglo Scottish Car Carrier', the 11.48am Edinburgh–Holloway, is depicted near Corby Glen on 21 July 1962 with English Electric Type 4 No D257 in charge. The cars travelled in specially adapted vans at the front of the train whilst the passengers relaxed in ordinary coaches that were marshalled at the rear. In addition to this train (and its corresponding down working) there was also a Holloway–Perth service, the 'Car Sleeper Limited', so people who wished to travel to and from Scotland without the hassle of driving were well catered for at this time. The leading vehicle is one of only four — classified CCT(E) — converted at Doncaster Works in 1960 from short-frame Gresley composite coaches. They carried BR numbers E96200-3 but with an 'E' suffix. In use no different from a standard GUV (the second vehicle in this consist), they were withdrawn in 1966. The next five vehicles — tiered car-carriers built by Newton Chambers in 1961 — had GRP (glass-reinforced plastic) bodies and roofs plus non-standard 6ft 9in-wheelbase bogies, which allowed the loading of two cars in the well between them; four more cars could be carried on the top deck. Classified TCV (Tiered Car Van), they were numbered E96286-99, again with an 'E' suffix for no apparent reason, being new vehicles. They were built to RIV standards (with the anchor symbol on the bodysides), having Westinghouse as well as vacuum brakes, though it is doubtful whether they ever ran on the Continent. The last would survive until 1987. *John Beckett*

A down express, believed to be the 16.20 King's Cross–Leeds/Bradford, is seen near
Corby Glen on 9 July 1966 with Brush Type 4 No D1579 in charge. This stretch of the
East Coast main line is very much a racing ground, without any curves of consequence
and only moderate gradients. The line climbs at around 1 in 200 all of the way from
Peterborough to Stoke Summit, about five miles south of Grantham. *John Beckett*

Above: A train from King's Cross to Newcastle (possibly the 9am departure, which included through carriages to Tyne Commission Quay) is depicted near Great Ponton in July 1962, with an immaculate BR/Sulzer 2,500hp Type 4 1Co-Co1 No D174 in command. Some 193 of these locomotives, which were commonly known as 'Peaks', were constructed by BR at Crewe and Derby works. The first 10, Nos D1-10, were non-standard 2,300hp machines, later becoming Class 44, which finished their days on freight work as described previously. The remainder were 2,500hp locomotives, and the bulk of these, known subsequently as Class 45 under the TOPS renumbering scheme, had Crompton Parkinson traction motors and control gear (like the first batch), but Nos D138-93 had Brush electrical equipment and later became Class 46. The locomotive seen here was one of the last-mentioned and must have been only a few days old when this shot

was taken. In its later years, as No 46 037, it became a celebrity machine, being the final member of the class to retain the old-style central headcode panel. Its career ended in spectacular fashion on 16 June 1984, when it went out in a blaze of glory on the Lickey Incline while powering the 10.35 Penzance–Leeds. It never recovered from the conflagration and was disposed of at Doncaster Works in January 1985. *John Beckett*

Right: English Electric Type 4 No D208 pauses at Grantham with an up express in September 1958. The locomotive appears to be almost brand-new and indeed it was, having officially entered service for the first time at Hornsey shed during the previous month. Perhaps it still retained some of the aroma of new paint! *Colour-Rail*

Left: The delightfully named Botany Bay signalbox, just north of Retford, presumably took its name from the nearby farm of the same name and not from a famous location on the Australian coastline! Its principal function was to control the crossing gates on the minor road that gave access to the farm. The bridge in the distance takes the main Retford–Doncaster road across the railway. In this picture, taken on 9 December 1974, an unidentified Class 47 approaches with the 10.50 Newcastle–King's Cross. *Hugh Ballantyne*

Left: The extent of cloud cover suggests the photographer has been lucky with the sun as 'Deltic' 3,300hp Co-Co No 55 019 *Royal Highland Fusilier* speeds along with the southbound 'Aberdonian', the 10.45 Aberdeen–King's Cross, on 9 July 1974. Pictured on the 1-in-200 rise south of Retford, the train comprises a mixture of Mk 1 and Mk 2 vehicles in blue/grey livery. Having emerged from Vulcan Foundry as No D9019 in December 1961, this locomotive ran nameless until September 1965, achieving the dubious distinction of being the last member of its class to remain unnamed. Based for most of its career at Edinburgh's Haymarket shed, it was withdrawn from York depot in December 1981, thereafter being fortunate enough to survive into preservation. *Hugh Ballantyne*

Right: Back in the early 1960s the arrival of a 'rare' Scottish Region-based Pacific for overhaul at The Plant (as Doncaster Works was known locally) caused unbelievable excitement among the local train-spotting fraternity. By 1969 steam was a thing of the past, and the shed was dominated entirely by diesel traction, as evinced by this shot of English Electric Type 3 (Class 37) Co-Co No D6935, taken on 15 June. Formerly allocated to the Western Region, the Type 3 was just over five years old at the time. In the background can be seen Brush Type 2 (Class 31) No 5853, whilst the 350hp diesel shunters (Class 08) are Nos D3663 and D3483.
Hugh Ballantyne

Right: With the shed's former coaling plant as a backdrop, diesel shunter No 2096 poses at Doncaster in a photograph taken the same day as the previous shot. Fitted with a 204hp Gardner engine and weighing 30 tons 16cwt, this locomotive could develop a tractive effort of 15,650lb. It was built at Doncaster in July 1960, but the light shunting duties for which it was designed disappeared rapidly as BR's freight business was rationalised, and it was destined to survive a mere 16 years in service, being withdrawn in December 1976 and scrapped at Doncaster three months later.
Hugh Ballantyne

The road overbridge just south of Doncaster station has long been a favourite location for railway photographers, and in this portrait one of the ubiquitous Class 47s, No 47 425, is seen accelerating away from its Doncaster stop with the 10.30 Edinburgh–King's Cross on 26 February 1974. The tracks veering off to the left in the foreground are those to Sheffield via Rotherham. No 47 425 began life as No D1533 and was one of the first batch of these locomotives to be constructed, being released from Brush's Loughborough works on 6 August 1963. It was renumbered under the TOPS scheme in March 1974, and the next major milestone in its life came on 15 April 1986, when it was named *Holbeck* by a retired driver from that well-known depot. The nameplates were, however, removed at Crewe in February 1991 and later fitted to No 47 634. No 47 425 was scrapped at Old Oak Common in April 1997. *Hugh Ballantyne*

Another photograph taken from the well known Doncaster vantage point features 'Deltic' No 55 002 *The King's Own Yorkshire Light Infantry* passing through the station with the up 'Flying Scotsman' on 1 March 1976. This locomotive entered traffic as No D9002 on 9 March 1961 at Gateshead shed, running nameless for more than two years until being ceremonially named at York station on 4 April 1963. The first member of its class to be repainted in corporate blue livery, in October 1966, it achieved further distinction on 5 May 1978 through powering the last locomotive-hauled 'Yorkshire Pullman'. In December 1980 it was outshopped in two-tone green livery and immediately gained celebrity status, which resulted in numerous appearances on railtours. It was officially withdrawn on 2 January 1982 and was subsequently preserved as part of the National Collection. *Hugh Ballantyne*

Left: North British Type 2 Bo-Bo No D6109 stands outside Doncaster Works in May 1959. Ten of these machines were ordered by the British Transport Commission as part of the Pilot Scheme for traction modernisation, and the first example rolled off NBL's Glasgow production line in 1958. Failures occurred during acceptance trials, and the class, which was destined for use on GN suburban services, was a source of constant headaches for operating and maintenance staff. BR failed to heed the early warnings, however, and ordered a further batch for use in East Anglia. In 1960 the entire class was transferred to Scotland, where the last of the 58 examples built entered service. Following the bankruptcy of North British in 1962 one example was re-engined with a 1,350hp Paxman Ventura power unit in an attempt to improve performance; later a further 19 locomotives were similarly modified, but despite this drastic action the class was eliminated in 1971. *Colour-Rail*

Left: Those were the days at Doncaster Works! In this photograph, taken in June 1967, can be seen a variety of types, including a couple of Brush Type 2 A1A-A1A locomotives (No D5817 nearer the camera), English Electric Type 3s and, in the background, the instantly recognisable shape of a 'Deltic', in this case No D9008 *The Green Howards*. The machine on the right is North British 800hp Bo-Bo No D8400. *Terry Phillips*

Spalding was once an important railway centre at the junction of the Peterborough–Grimsby (East Lincolnshire), March–Doncaster (Great Northern & Great Eastern Joint) and ex-Midland & Great Northern Leicester–Norwich/Great Yarmouth lines. However, all of these were secondary routes passing through predominantly rural areas, so their future was far from secure when BR came under pressure to reduce its deficit. The M&GN, which served few intermediate places of any importance, was an early casualty, closing in March 1959. The East Lincolnshire line was largely closed in October 1970, but the Peterborough–Spalding section reopened in June 1971 with financial support from the local authority — an event that would lead to the later closure of the GN/GE Joint line south of Spalding. In the mid-1970s Spalding's regular train service was extremely meagre, comprising just three weekday services in each direction on the Joint line and a mere two daily trains to Peterborough. However, a notable exception to this depressing picture came on the day of the town's tulip parade, when many extra trains ran from far and wide, and the station's facilities were stretched to the limit, returning passengers not being allowed into the station until their trains were available to board. Seen awaiting departure on 11 May 1974 is the 18.10 return excursion to Eastbourne, formed of two Southern Region '6B' DEMUs, No 1037 leading. *Terry Phillips*

A Skegness-bound DMU awaits departure from Firsby station on 6 March 1970. The train is standing in Platform 1, which was bi-directional; this method of operation was a legacy of the days when it was used by Spilsby branch services, although the last passenger train from Firsby to Spilsby had run on 10 September 1939. Despite the fact that the station served only a small village, a fair-sized building was provided with a loop platform on the up side and a goods shed, part of which is just visible. Note the remains of the Great Northern Railway overall roof, which survived until the end. The station was located at the northern end of the triangle where the Skegness branch joined the East Lincolnshire line; when the latter was partially closed only the south curve remained open, and Firsby station was closed, but at least the line to the 'bracing' resort of Skegness was saved. *Roy Patterson*

The view north at Mablethorpe on 11 April 1970, with a two-car DMU standing in the station after arrival with a train from Willoughby. In the days before cheap Continental holidays and private motoring became the norm for the masses, the typical British family spent their annual holiday at the seaside. Mablethorpe was a favourite destination for many people, especially those living in the East Midlands and South Yorkshire, and the station was doubtless a hive of activity on summer Saturdays in the 1950s and '60s. By the time of this picture, however, such traffic had become a thing of the past, and Mablethorpe lost its remaining services when it was removed from the railway map later the same year. *Terry Phillips*

Above: Even the most ardent fan of the Doncaster–Cleethorpes line would surely not claim that it is one of the most attractive in Great Britain but it does have some points of interest, especially at Keadby where the line crosses the Stainforth & Keadby Canal and two other waterways, including the River Trent, in barely over a mile. On 21 April 1963 the Railway Enthusiasts' Club chartered a two-car DMU for a tour of North Lincolnshire, and here the train is seen during a stop to enable participants to explore the scenic delights of Keadby. For many the highlight of the tour, which started at Doncaster, was probably a steam-hauled brake-van trip up the Scunthorpe–Whitton branch as far as Winterton, a journey that had not been possible in a passenger train since services were withdrawn back in July 1925! The tour also visited New Holland and Barton-on-Humber and other lines in the Grimsby area before returning to Doncaster via Barnetby. The DMU was clearly well turned out for the trip and sparkles in the spring sunshine whilst the colourful barges in the foreground add further interest to the scene. *Roy Patterson*

Right: Later the same day the railtour featured in the previous picture visited Immingham Dock station, where two members of BR staff are seen apparently endeavouring to remove the train's headboard. The vehicle nearest the camera is Driving Trailer Composite (DTCL) No E56003, one of a batch built at Derby Carriage Works in 1956 for Lincoln-area services. The station here was a terminus, with basic facilities situated adjacent to the dock, the nearest residential area being the village of Immingham; however, the station was inconveniently situated in relation to the village and is unlikely to have attracted any local traffic other than dock workers. The line northwards to New Holland lost its passenger services in June 1963, whilst the route westwards to Ulceby lasted until October 1969. *Roy Patterson*

The view at Ely on 22 May 1971, with the 09.25 service to Cambridge awaiting departure. The leading vehicle, a Driving Motor Brake Second (DMBS), was constructed by D. Wickham & Co Ltd as part of an order for just five two-car units that nevertheless took a year to complete. The sets were of revolutionary construction (at least for use in Great Britain) and dispensed with the need for a conventional underframe; instead a skeleton, capable of withstanding the load and other stresses, was built up from solid drawn square steel tubing and, in effect, formed a box girder. The design was evolved for use in South America, strength being combined with lightweight construction. The weight of the skeleton was 5.3 tons, and a complete two-car unit weighed no more than 48 tons. The vehicles also had corrugated steel floors, aluminium body panelling and unusual but stylish art-deco interiors. Each unit consisted of a DMBS, powered by two 150hp Leyland engines, and a Driving Trailer Composite (DTC), giving a total seating capacity of 16 first class and 109 second. The type was represented at the Modern Railway Travel Exhibition, held from 28 to 30 June 1957 at Battersea Wharf goods depot, where various examples of diesel locomotives and modern rolling stock were displayed. The DMBS, No E50415, was exhibited as a complete vehicle, whilst a DTC was shown in skeleton form. It will be noted from the picture that the letters 'LW' are stencilled within the 'blue square' coupling-code symbol. Not all types of unit had the same control system, and only those that were compatible (and thus marked with the same coupling code) could run together. 'LW' indicated that the set was of lightweight construction, and thus there were restrictions on the tail load that could be hauled. By early 1971 there were only two Wickham units left in traffic, and all had gone by October of that year. Of the three previously withdrawn, two went to Trinidad and the other, consisting of DMBS No E50416 and DTC No E56171, was converted and renumbered for use as the Eastern Region General Manager's saloon (as seen opposite), surviving in this role until 1980. *Terry Phillips*

Above: As described opposite, one of the Wickham units was converted to the Eastern Region General Manager's saloon, being seen here in this guise in the late 1970s. Conversion involved extensive alterations, including the installation of kitchen equipment where the guard's van had been located, the plating over of some doorways and the straightening of the gutter arrangement above the cab windows. The vehicles concerned were Nos E50416 (DMBS) and E56171 (DTC), these being renumbered DB975005 and DB975006 respectively. This unit was the last of the 'Wickhams' to run on BR and continued in departmental service until 1980. It was purchased for private preservation and was stored initially at the Chasewater Railway. The unit was stripped of all remaining blue asbestos prior to moving to the Midland Railway Centre, where it was magnificently restored to original condition, this work being supported by a Heritage Lottery Fund (HLF) grant of £129,000 — the first time the HLF had authorised a grant for a DMU restoration project. In 2003 it moved to the Llangollen Railway, where it remains at the time of writing. *John Hayward*

Inset: The roomy interior of one of the Wickham coaches when still in departmental use. *John Hayward*

The distinctive (but probably little-photographed) overall roof of Grimsby station provides the backdrop to this picture of a Doncaster–Cleethorpes local train departing on 19 August 1976. This must have been the photographer's lucky day, because the train was booked to be formed of a DMU, which had presumably expired, and a much more photogenic substitute was provided at short notice. The leading locomotive is Class 31 No 31 301, whilst the train engine is classmate No 31 417. The former was originally No D5834 and entered traffic in March 1962, whilst the latter, which entered service in August of the same year, was previously No D5856. With two locomotives hauling just three coaches the passengers no doubt experienced some exceptionally lively running. *Hugh Ballantyne*

Right: On 27 June 1976 the Main Line Steam Trust, the society behind the preservation of the Great Central Railway between Loughborough and Leicester, operated a railtour from Leicester to New Holland Pier using a Swindon-built 'Cross Country' unit. The day out included a trip on the *Lincoln Castle*, which at that time was the last coal-fired paddle steamer in Great Britain and was still in regular use on the BR ferry service from New Holland to Hull. In this picture the DMU is seen passing through New Holland Town as empty coaching stock prior to forming the 18.05 return excursion to the East Midlands. Displayed in the cab window, 'EP 596' was the unit's set number, 'EP' representing Etches Park, Derby, where a considerable number of these units was based at the time. A total of 65 of these sets was built between 1958 and 1961, mainly for Western Region services, such as those from Cardiff to Bristol and South Wales to Birmingham. In addition to a somewhat austere front end these sets boasted a small buffet in the centre car and a very large brake van in one of the motor coaches. Strangely the latter vehicle — rather than the trailer, which would have provided a better ride with reduced noise and vibration — also contained the first-class seating. Swindon always insisted on doing things differently! The last of these sets survived until October 1989, and it is regrettable that just one buffet coach survives in preservation. *Terry Phillips*

Right: A four-car DMU rake of Derby 'Heavyweights' stands in the up platform at New Holland Town in 1966. The branch to Barton-on-Humber formed a triangular junction with the 'main' line to Grimsby just beyond the level crossing gates. Note the very generous canopy provided for passengers on the up platform. *David Mitchell*

Above: Apparently waiting to depart for Barton-on-Humber, a two-car DMU stands at New Holland Pier on 19 August 1976 after arriving as the 14.01 train from Cleethorpes. Note the indescribably shabby state of the station premises, which gives the impression that regional management had forgotten about this remote outpost of their territory; apart from the fact that the station building had not been repainted for years, half of the canopy roof appears to be missing. Berthed on the centre road are wagons containing fuel for the *Lincoln Castle. Hugh Ballantyne*

Right: A two-car DMU arrives at Barton-on-Humber in the spring of 1966. The station buildings appear to be dirty and neglected and are hardly a good advertisement for rail travel. At the time of writing this short branch is still in use, served by a local service to and from Cleethorpes. *David Mitchell*

Left: The lovely vintage signalbox at Habrough, with its set of crossing gates, semaphore signalling and apparently intact station building with dark blue running-in board are reminders of times past, when railways were really full of interest. If a steam train had suddenly appeared in the distance it would not have looked out of place, but by the date of this picture, 19 July 1969, a diesel-hauled train or DMU was the best that could be hoped for! Here a DMU forming a Cleethorpes–Retford local service eases towards its stop. *John Hayward*

Left: In times gone by slow-moving cross-country freight trains on the Grimsby–Sheffield route crossed the East Coast main line on the level at Retford, which was a permanent headache for the operating authorities and, no doubt, a source of many delays. The layout permitted passenger trains on the former line to use the ECML platforms, but they also made conflicting movements with main-line traffic. In the early 1960s BR sought to eliminate this operational nightmare by building a 'flyunder' for Sheffield-line trains together with new, low-level platforms that were separate from the main part of the station. In this photograph, also taken on 19 July 1969, a two-car DMU waits in the low-level part of Retford station. *John Hayward*

If asked to name ports on the East Coast most people would suggest Felixstowe, Lowestoft or Immingham, but very few would be likely to identify the smaller port of Boston, which is in any case a place much better known for its famous church tower, known locally as 'Boston Stump'. In this picture Class 03 diesel shunter No 03 026 has just passed over the swing bridge in the docks area and is about to cross the busy A16 main road, this being the principal north-south road through the town. The level-crossing gates are closed to road traffic, and no doubt motorists delayed by such shunting and transfer operations had a few caustic comments to make. Note the dainty Great Northern Railway somersault signal. No 03 026, among the earliest of these 204hp machines to be constructed, was turned out by Swindon Works in September 1958 as No D2026. Following withdrawal in February 1983 it was broken up by C. F. Booth Ltd of Rotherham in April 1984. *Hugh Ballantyne*

Left: The splendid station building with its tower and ornate chimney-stacks, the distinctive signalbox with its strange 'extension' and busy city-centre level crossing … there is no mistaking Lincoln Central station. In this photograph, dating from 16 September 1961, English Electric Type 4 1Co-Co1 No D352 is seen passing light-engine over the crossing at the north end of the station. At the time a mere two months old, as evinced by its very clean condition, this locomotive would have an unremarkable career, but on Easter Saturday 1983, as No 40 152, it gained a place in history by powering the southbound 'Royal Scot'. During that Easter weekend the West Coast main line was out of action due to extensive engineering works, trains being diverted via the Settle–Carlisle line; most were worked by Brush Class 47s, but Kingmoor depot was obviously desperate for motive power, hence the use of this locomotive. *Colour-Rail*

Above: A view of Shirebrook diesel depot on a gloomy 8 September 1968, with a number of Brush Type 2s present. This was a Sunday, hence the depot roads are almost fully occupied. The locomotive nearest the camera is No D5835, still sporting green livery albeit with a full yellow end. This machine was released for traffic in April 1962 and later became No 31 302 under the TOPS system. Shirebrook depot, situated in the middle of a tangle of lines between Nottingham and Worksop, replaced the old Langwith Junction steam shed, which had closed in December 1966. Its principal purpose was to provide power for the many coal trains that ran throughout the Nottinghamshire coalfield. Shirebrook may have been an obscure depot 'off the beaten track' of many enthusiasts, but its profile was raised in the late 1960s/ early 1970s when the prototype 4,000hp Co-Co No HS4000 *Kestrel* was a regular visitor. This machine, then allocated to Tinsley, undertook test trials in various parts of the country, but most of its time in revenue-earning service was spent hauling 1,600-ton coal trains between Shirebrook and March (Whitemoor Yard). *Terry Phillips*

Above: Few pictures of trains in the Sheffield area were submitted for consideration for this album, but here is the 14.52 Sheffield–St Pancras train awaiting departure behind Class 45 No 45 002 on 18 August 1973. This working actually appeared in the public timetable as two separate trains, the 14.52 from Sheffield to Nottingham and 15.58 from Nottingham to St Pancras, as there was a faster 15.00 Sheffield–St Pancras service via the Erewash Valley line. Built at Derby Works in May 1961 as No D29, No 45 002 remained in traffic until September 1984 and was eventually scrapped by MC Metals at Glasgow in November 1988. The locomotive partially visible on the extreme right is BR/Sulzer Type 2 No 7501. *Chris Evans*

Above right: English Electric Type 4 1Co-Co1 No D200 stands at Liverpool Street at the head of a demonstration run to Norwich on 18 April 1958. This locomotive was amongst the earliest main-line diesels built under the 1955 British Railways Modernisation Plan, and ultimately a further 199 similar locomotives were constructed. The class was associated with the initial dieselisation of the London–Norwich line, and No D200 was based at a number of different depots in East Anglia before August 1967, when it moved to the LMR. Renumbered 40 122 under TOPS, it was initially withdrawn in August 1981

but was reinstated to traffic on 24 April 1983, using the power unit and bogies from sister locomotive No 40 076; work on the locomotive, which included restoration to BR green livery, was carried out as apprentice training at Toton depot. No 40 122 ran until 16 April 1988, when it hauled a special from Liverpool Street to Norwich and then on to York, prior to entering the National Railway Museum. *Colour-Rail*

Right: Brush Type 4 Co-Co No 1530 arrives at Liverpool Street with the 11.40 from Norwich on 14 August 1969. This locomotive had entered traffic on 15 July 1963 as No D1530 and between October 1966 and December 1974 was allocated to Stratford depot. It is seen here still in original two-tone green livery but with the addition of full yellow ends, these replacing the small warning panels originally applied below the windscreens. Liverpool Street station would be extensively rebuilt between 1985 and 1992, and the scene at the platform ends is very different today. As part of the redevelopment the nearby Broad Street station was closed in June 1986, and for a while thereafter certain trains on the North London line ran to and from Liverpool Street. *Hugh Ballantyne*

In overall Rail blue, English Electric Type 3 Co-Co No 6916 passes through Chelmsford with an up train of brake-fitted 21-ton coal hoppers on a glorious May evening in 1972. Being of later construction, the locomotive was not fitted with nose-end doors and therefore has a central four-character headcode panel rather than two characters in separate boxes mounted each side of the doors. Delivered new to Landore in January 1964, it was allocated to Stratford between September 1971 and March 1973. It was renumbered 37 216 under TOPS in 1974 and later, in March 1992, was named *Great Eastern* and returned to green livery for a period. At the time of writing it is undergoing restoration on the Pontypool & Blaenavon Railway. *Terry Phillips*

The driver looks back as Brush Type 4 Co-Co No 1992 eases out of Chelmsford station with the 07.37 Yarmouth Vauxhall–Liverpool Street, the single-aspect colour-light signal having already returned to red. The locomotive was delivered as No D1992 on 15 March 1966 and at the time this photograph was taken, in May 1972, was allocated to Gateshead depot; perhaps it had been requisitioned by the operating authorities on the Great Eastern section to make up a shortfall of suitable motive power. Renumbered 47 290 under the TOPS scheme, it would be rebuilt in 2004 with a General Motors engine as No 57 316 *FAB 1*. It is now part of Virgin Trains' 'Thunderbird' fleet (its 'name' being the registration of the vehicle featured in the *Thunderbirds* television series), created primarily to provide strategically located rescue locomotives for failed trains. *Terry Phillips*

Above: Brush Type 2 A1A-A1A No D5563 enters Witham station with a down freight on 7 August 1969. The first 20 members of this class were built under the Modernisation Plan's Pilot Scheme, intended to permit evaluation of various designs of diesel locomotive supplied mainly by private industry, although in the event the headlong rush into 'dieselisation' as a panacea for BR's deficit meant that further large orders were placed before the assessment took place. The Brush Type 2 was, however, very successful, a further 243 being built, although the original Mirrlees engines were replaced from the mid-1960s by a more powerful (1,470hp) English Electric type. Delivered in November 1959, No D5563 would be renumbered 31 145 under TOPS and withdrawn in August 1997. Although a few of these locomotives remain at the time of writing, the mixed freight comprising four-wheeled wagons as illustrated here is now very much a part of history. *Colour-Rail*

Right: The Modernisation Plan was criticised in some quarters for being little more than a replacement of steam locomotives with more modern traction. As if to confirm that suggestion, Brush 1,365hp Type 2 A1A-A1A No D5527 is here seen arriving at Kelvedon with an Ipswich–Liverpool Street working on 20 May 1961. Clearly prominent are the headcode discs that were fitted to early diesel locomotives, following time-honoured steam practice, and the coaching stock, which includes pre-nationalisation designs. The first and second vehicles are respectively Thompson and Gresley types. Further modernisation is underway, electrification gantries having been erected, although the catenary has yet to be installed. Telegraph wires and gas lighting on stations were, in 1961, still commonplace across the entire railway network. *Colour-Rail*

Above: Here seen resting between duties at Colchester on 3 April 1974 are two types of diesel shunting locomotive. On the left is BR-built 0-6-0 No 2027, fitted with a 204hp Gardner engine, whilst on the right, retaining its 'D' prefix, is BR/English Electric 350hp 0-6-0 No D3112. The former locomotive was built in 1958 and, as No 03 027, would remain in BR service until 1976; after further use by a private industrial owner in Kent it entered preservation and at the time of writing is based at Peak Rail in Derbyshire. No D3112 was a member of the most numerous class of diesel locomotive ever built in Great Britain, more than a thousand being constructed. The earlier locomotives predated the 1957 numbering scheme that introduced the 'D' prefix, this example was built in 1955 as No 13112. Designated Class 08 under the TOPS scheme, these shunters still number in the hundreds, but No D3112 (latterly 08 087) was withdrawn in 1979 and cut up at Swindon Works the following year. *Hugh Ballantyne*

Right: On 27 March 1972 Brush Type 4 Co-Co No 1582 calls at Colchester with the 12.30 Liverpool Street–Norwich express. Still in original two-tone green, the locomotive has its number applied in a later style, which was used in conjunction with corporate blue livery. The train consists of a set of blue-and-grey Mk 1s, presenting a neat appearance. Brush Type 4s were generally diagrammed for the principal London–Norwich trains, but use of English Electric Type 3s was also commonplace at this time. Delivered on 16 May 1964 as No D1582, this locomotive was allocated to Stratford at the time of the photograph but three months later was transferred to the London Midland Region; renumbered 47 462 under TOPS, it survived until March 2003, when it was cut up at Toton. *Terry Phillips*

Left: Brush Type 4 Co-Co No 47 010 leaves Colchester on 3 April 1974 with the 13.30 Liverpool Street–Norwich, the formation including a number of Mk 2 vehicles. No 47 010 had been delivered in August 1963 as No D1537 and renumbered in February 1974. Since June 1972 it had been allocated to Stratford, where it was to remain for a further six years before being reallocated to Finsbury Park. Withdrawn in January 1993, it was cut up by C. F. Booth of Rotherham in December of the same year. *Hugh Ballantyne*

Below left: A train of Ford containers — very likely *en route* from Felixstowe Docks to the Ford Motor Co's plant at Halewood — climbs the grade through Colchester station in the up direction behind Brush Type 4 (Class 47) Co-Co No 1758, in two-tone green with all yellow ends. In this May 1972 view the station appears to be busy, with the 17.22 Liverpool Street–Clacton/ Walton-on-Naze service, formed of 'AM9' (later Class 309) stock, in the down loop platform, whilst the down main-line signals have been cleared for another train. Delivered on 23 May 1964 as No D1758, the locomotive would be renumbered 47 164 under the TOPS scheme in December 1973. Since January 1970 it had been based at Stratford depot, where it remained until November 1977. Having gained Rail-blue livery, it was to spend its final few months at Stratford adorned with a silver roof and a full-height Union Jack on each side to mark HM The Queen's Silver Jubilee — a distinction shared with No 47 163. Successive modifications would see it further renumbered as 47 571 and then 47 822 before a rebuild in January 2003 as one of the Virgin 'Thunderbird' fleet of Class 57/3s, No 57 305 *Alan Tracy*. Continuing a long and varied career, the locomotive remains in service at the time of writing. *Terry Phillips*

Brush Type 2 (Class 31) A1A-A1A No 5518 brings the up 'Day Continental', the 18.33 Harwich Parkeston Quay–Liverpool Street, past a fine array of semaphore signals and through Manningtree station on a Saturday evening in June 1972. The locomotive had been given a white roof, which was applied by Stratford depot in 1969 prior to use on the Victoria–Tattenham Corner Derby Day Royal Train, as well as the BR double arrow, generally reserved for locomotives and multiple-units in the corporate blue (or blue and grey) livery introduced in the mid-1960s. Note, on the up platform, the Eastern Region blue running-in board; also the station name on the platform light, a feature that was commonplace at the time. Renumbered 31 101 under the TOPS scheme, the locomotive would be withdrawn in January 1993 and survives today in preservation on the Battlefield Line in Leicestershire. *Terry Phillips*

Left: On a fine summer's evening in 1972 the stock for the 18.50 to Liverpool Street is brought into Ipswich station by English Electric Type 3 Co-Co No 6735. On account of the end doors the locomotive is equipped with a split four-character headcode display. These doors were a feature of earlier diesel locomotives but were soon taken out of use and sealed; later locomotives were built without them, as illustrated elsewhere in this book. Delivered (as No D6735) on 17 April 1962 and allocated initially to Hull Dairycoates, this locomotive would be renumbered 37 035 under the TOPS scheme. Stored unserviceable in September 1996, it was cut up in January 2000, by Booth's of Rotherham. *Terry Phillips*

Above: Brush Type 2 A1A-A1A No D5566 awaits departure from Norwich Thorpe on 13 March 1965 with the 1.40pm to Liverpool Street. The locomotive is in green livery with the warning panel below the windscreens, as applied prior to the introduction of the all-yellow ends that were shortly to become standard, while the white stripes above the bogies and halfway up the bodyside helped improve the rather box-like appearance; as the photograph was taken before the introduction of corporate Rail blue and grey, the locomotive has the BR lion-and-wheel crest. Since the closure to passengers in 1959 of the ex-Midland & Great Northern Railway Norwich City station Thorpe has been the only passenger station in Norwich. It did not lose its suffix, however, until May 1969, Norwich City station having remained open for freight traffic until February of that year. *Colour-Rail*

In a classic shot taken in the Rail-blue era English Electric Type 3 (Class 37) Co-Co No 37 078 — delivered on 29 October 1962 as No D6778 — begins its journey to London with the 13.46 Norwich–Liverpool Street on 18 September 1975. The train is formed largely of Mk 1 and non-air-conditioned Mk 2 stock. The sixth vehicle is a former Pullman parlour car, built by Metropolitan-Cammell in 1960 and made redundant on the East Coast route in 1971; used on the Great Eastern as Open Firsts, such coaches were frequently marshalled, as here, next to a catering vehicle and were used for serving meals. On the left of the picture can be seen 204hp diesel shunter No 03 020 on station-pilot duty, whilst behind the train are three Cravens DMUs. In the background the station buildings and the spire of Norwich Cathedral complete a fascinating scene.
Hugh Ballantyne

In addition to the hourly service of express trains between London and Norwich via Ipswich there were a number of trains that ran via Cambridge, although because of the longer journey times these were rarely attractive to through passengers. In this picture, taken on 4 September 1971, English Electric Type 3 Co-Co No 6729 is about to couple to the stock of the 10.23 Summer Saturdays-only Norwich–Liverpool Street via Cambridge. Delivered in October 1961 as No D6729, the locomotive was allocated initially to Stratford but by the time of this picture was based at March. Although the photograph was taken some years after the introduction of corporate blue, maroon coaching stock could still be found in East Anglia on seasonal strengthening duties; one such vehicle, a Mk 1 Open Second, can be seen in the carriage sidings on the left, displaying the carriage-stock version of the British Railways crest. Note that the station is still described on the running-in board (right) as Norwich Thorpe. *Terry Phillips*

Above: Photographed a short distance in to its journey, the 13.20 Norwich–Yarmouth Vauxhall passes Wensum Junction, Norwich, on 4 September 1971. The train consists of two twin DMU sets, the leading unit (further from the camera) having being built by Metropolitan-Cammell, the other by the Gloucester Railway Carriage & Wagon Co. The photograph was taken from the 08.40 Summer Saturdays-only Leeds City–Yarmouth Vauxhall service, which was being held on the Norwich avoiding line — known as the Wensum curve — to allow the DMUs to precede it. At this time the local services in East Anglia were almost universally in the hands of DMUs. Many stations were unstaffed, and conductor-guard working was the norm, services being marketed under the generic name of 'Paytrain'. Gloucester sets, which became Class 100 under TOPS, did not appear in East Anglia until the late 1960s, following traffic decline and line closures in Scotland.
Terry Phillips

Right: As passengers gather for the next up local train to Norwich, Brush Type 2 A1A-A1A No 5630 passes through Brundall with the 07.07 Summer Saturdays-only Chesterfield–Yarmouth Vauxhall on a glorious summer's day, 15 July 1972. Although by this time officially unstaffed, the station looks well cared for, with a fine display of roses. Beyond Brundall the line from Norwich splits into two, the more northerly route continuing as a single line to Yarmouth via Acle, and the original, southerly line giving access to both Yarmouth and Lowestoft via Reedham. Expresses from Norwich to Yarmouth took either route, as dictated by traffic conditions. Significant improvements, such as track circuiting and partial resignalling with colour lights, were made to the Acle line in 1960 following closure of the former Midland & Great Northern line to Yarmouth and the resultant diversion of holiday traffic to the former Great Eastern lines.
Terry Phillips

Left: Drewry 204hp diesel shunting locomotive No D2210 is seen at work at Yarmouth Vauxhall on 29 August 1967. This class was introduced in 1952 for use on lines (*e.g.* with tight curves) that could not accommodate a 350hp shunter. Although these machines were supplied by the Drewry Car Co, this was largely a sales organisation, and production was sub-contracted to the Vulcan Foundry and Robert Stephenson & Hawthorn; No D2210 was constructed by the former. This example, one of two allocated to Yarmouth for working the harbour tramway, had enclosed wheels and motion and was fitted with a cowcatcher; a number of other lines were worked by similar locomotives, the most notable being the Wisbech & Upwell Tramway. Although classified 04 under TOPS, the type would be extinct by 1971, before renumbering commenced.
The Yarmouth Docks line, built to connect the Midland & Great Northern Railway's Beach station with the Great Eastern's Vauxhall station and the principal quays, was to close with effect from 1 January 1976.
Terry Phillips

Left: A Derby Lightweight DMU departs from Great Chesterford in June 1966 on what appears to be a Cambridge–Bishop's Stortford local working. Note the somewhat plain station building, the staggered platforms and the rural location. This line has since been electrified, and the platforms have been extended, now being nearly opposite each other and connected by a footbridge; the down loop, seen here, has disappeared, this area being partially occupied by the extended down platform. The Derby Lightweight cars were the first DMU stock introduced by British Railways, having been ordered in November 1952. Constructed at Derby Works in 1954, the first vehicles entered service between Leeds and Bradford in June of that year, predating the Modernisation Plan, and in 1955 a further batch was delivered for use in East Anglia. The class was a great success, and ultimately 217 cars were built. However, aside from a few in departmental service all had disappeared by 1969, and the type was never given a TOPS classification. *Colour-Rail*

In an evocative scene recorded on 14 May 1960, Brush Type 2 A1A-A1A No D5518 approaches Shelford station with an up mixed freight. Featured elsewhere in this book, the locomotive is seen here with its original headcode discs, destined to be replaced by a four-character display in 1967 following accident damage. The train is of interest through having a fitted head, the leading vehicles being equipped with vacuum brakes (operated from the locomotive), whilst the open wagons at the rear appear to be mostly unfitted.

The two leading wagons are carrying wooden-bodied containers, these representing an early attempt to mitigate the problem of transfer to road vehicles for final delivery. Behind the train can be seen a goods shed and some rail-served industrial premises, with a ventilated van present. Such methods of freight distribution have long since been consigned to history. *Colour-Rail*

Left: English Electric Type 3 Co-Co No D6703 stands at one of the bay platforms at the north end of Cambridge station on 16 June 1962, by which date steam working had been all but eliminated from East Anglia. Unfortunately the train details are not recorded, but the picture nevertheless serves as a fascinating record of the early diesel era. The leading coach is of Gresley design, whilst in the background, framed by a fine array of lower-quadrant signals, can be seen a Metropolitan-Cammell DMU and a 204hp diesel shunter. The former has the warning 'whiskers' which at the time were considered an adequate aid to visibility, whilst the shunter has not yet gained the black and yellow chevrons that were applied to such locomotives from around this time. New to Stratford on 28 December 1960, No D6703 was purchased in April 1998 by the Class 37 Locomotive Group and is today preserved in its TOPS guise as No 37 003. *Colour-Rail*

Left: In a scene recorded 10 years later, on Saturday 15 July 1972, Brush Type 2 A1A-A1A No 5529 arrives at Cambridge with the 15.15 from Birmingham New Street. This would normally have been a DMU working, but on summer Saturdays a number of local and cross-country trains were regularly locomotive-hauled, enabling capacity to be increased on the train in question and releasing multiple-unit stock to strengthen other DMU services. By this date the signal gantry seen in the previous photograph had been replaced by a rather more simple arrangement! The signalbox in the background remains, however. Maroon coaches can be seen both in the train and in the carriage sidings on the right. The leading (blue and grey) coach is a Mk 1 Corridor Composite (CK); the second compartment from the rear is equipped with a hinged window to enable a passenger on a stretcher to be carried onto or off a train — an arrangement known to railwaymen as 'direct access'. *Terry Phillips*

Ely, in the Cambridgeshire Fens, is a major railway junction, which today has five routes radiating from it, to Norwich, Ipswich, Cambridge, King's Lynn and Peterborough; a further line — to St Ives — lost its passenger services as long ago as 1931. On the sunny winter's morning of 13 February 1971 a DMU, forming the 10.54 from Cambridge to Leicester, has just entered the down platform loop, although the destination on the leading vehicle is shown erroneously as 'Peterborough'. The two-car set consists of a Driving Trailer Composite built by Cravens Ltd and, at the rear, a Gloucester Railway Carriage & Wagon Co-built Motor Brake Second. The heavier underframe of the latter car is readily apparent. The leading car appears to have had its first-class saloon, which would have been immediately behind the driver, downgraded to second; it was also amongst the earlier cars built, having four marker lights incorporated in the front end rather than the two lights and two-digit headcode panels fitted to later sets. Cravens produced a total of 405 railcars, all being delivered between 1956 and 1959, the last survivors being withdrawn from passenger service in 1988. Note the green diesel shunter, No D2006; also the evidence of considerable freight activity in the background.
Terry Phillips

The beginning of the 1970s saw some enhancements to the cross-country services running between Norwich/Cambridge and Birmingham via Peterborough. Not only was there an increase in the number of trains operated, but also the principal services were allocated to three-car 'Cross Country' units built at Swindon Works between 1958 and 1961. This picture, taken on 22 May 1971, shows one of these units forming the 08.10 Norwich–Birmingham New Street train at Ely, where the train reversed. The vehicle nearest the camera is a Driving Motor Second containing 68 seats. These units were built for the Western and Scottish regions, but the former had transferred a number to the London Midland Region in the 1960s, and some years later they were made available for these workings. Under the TOPS scheme the 'Cross Country' units became Class 120, the last vehicles surviving until 1989. Ely's status as an important junction is apparent from the presence of three other trains in the station, that on the left being the 07.33 Harwich Parkeston Quay–Manchester Piccadilly service, with which the 08.10 was booked to make a double connection. *Terry Phillips*

English Electric Type 3 (Class 37) Co-Co No 6712 pulls into the up loop platform at Ely on 15 July 1972 with the 14.40 Manchester Piccadilly–Harwich Parkeston Quay service. The locomotive remains in green livery, albeit with the addition of full yellow ends, but the coaches are in corporate Rail blue and grey. This train was noteworthy at the time for the regular inclusion of a Gresley-designed buffet car, being one of the last regular workings for such a vehicle — on this occasion No E9122E. Delivered on 10 March 1961 as No D6712, the locomotive was allocated initially to Stratford depot, where, after a number of transfers, it returned in 1971. The Manchester–Harwich boat train was known unofficially as the 'North Country Continental' and had been introduced in 1883 following the opening of the then new Parkeston Quay. At the time of this photograph it ran via the Great Northern & Great Eastern Joint line through Spalding, but from 7 May 1973 it was diverted via Peterborough and Nottingham. Regrettably this interesting train no longer runs. *Terry Phillips*

Below: Brush Type 2 A1A-A1A No 5621 arrives at Thetford with the 07.05 Summer Saturdays-only Chesterfield–Yarmouth Vauxhall train on 4 September 1971. The locomotive would initially be renumbered 31 197 under TOPS, later becoming 31 423 when fitted with electric train heating apparatus. Nominally running non-stop from Retford (!), the train was one of a number of Summer Saturday-dated trains that called at Thetford. In this view the station retains ER blue signs, telegraph wires and poles and what appears to be a Great Eastern Railway seat, while adding to the scene are the traditional canopies. *Terry Phillips*

Right: The BR/Sulzer Type 2 Bo-Bo had its origins in the Modernisation Plan Pilot Scheme. Incorporating the Sulzer 6LDA28 engine, ultimately no fewer than 478 of these versatile locomotives were built in various BR workshops and by Beyer Peacock between 1958 and 1967. The first 151 were to become TOPS Class 24 and generated 1,160hp, whilst the later Class 25s were 1,250hp machines. Here one of the latter, No D7588, heads through Thetford on 4 September 1971 with the Summer Saturdays-only 07.55 Walsall–Yarmouth Vauxhall. The end doors fitted to the locomotive, by this time sealed out of use, are clearly visible. The train appears well patronised, and seat regulation was in force; this advance-booking arrangement was applied to certain popular holiday trains and assisted in controlling overloading. Above the locomotive can be seen a 'pill box', one of many installed as part of the defence measures taken in World War 2. Although some members of Class 25 were to remain in traffic until 1987, No D7588 was

not so fortunate, being withdrawn in October 1980 and subsequently cut up at BREL Swindon. *Terry Phillips*

Below right: Headed by a pair of BR/Sulzer Type 2 (Class 25) Bo-Bo locomotives, the 14.20 Summer Saturdays-only Yarmouth Vauxhall–Derby train makes an unadvertised stop at Thetford. The leading locomotive is No 7607, the second, in two-tone green livery similar to that applied to the Brush Type 4s, is No 7564. Both locomotives have the final style of cab fitted to this class following the decision to dispense with end access doors; consequently the middle section of the windscreen is larger than on earlier locomotives. The result is a much neater appearance, which is enhanced further by the removal of the air intakes from the bodysides to the roof. Although the overwhelming majority of coaches were by this time in corporate blue and grey, for a number of summers in the early 1970s the operating authorities at Derby were able to assemble a train of all-maroon coaching stock, which was then booked to run for the whole season on a specific service. In 1972 the stock worked out on the 08.30 Derby–Yarmouth Vauxhall and returned as the 14.20, as seen here. It should be noted that the 'Vauxhall' suffix was dropped in the timetable effective from 1 May 1972, and since 16 May 1989 the official name has been Great Yarmouth, but despite these changes railway staff — and local people, no doubt — still refer to the station as Yarmouth Vauxhall. *Terry Phillips*

Left: The 14.52 Colchester–Sudbury service, formed of a two-car Cravens DMU, calls at Chappel & Wakes Colne on 27 March 1972. The number 50 in the windscreen is a local set number, this being applied to most DMUs based in East Anglia at this time as part of an effort, wherever possible, to make up sets with all vehicles built by the same manufacturer. The line from Marks Tey to Sudbury, opened on 2 June 1849, was later extended to Haverhill via Long Melford, this section opening on 9 August 1865. The 1960s was a period in which many lines and stations closed — following publication of the notorious Beeching Report — but consent for closure of the Marks Tey–Sudbury section was refused. After a period of some uncertainty the threat to withdraw the passenger service was lifted in the mid-1970s. Chappel was also the junction for the Colne Valley line, which ran via Halstead to Haverhill, but passenger services were withdrawn in 1962, the final goods trains running in 1965. In this view stock from the embryonic East Anglian Railway Museum can be seen behind the disused southbound platform. *Terry Phillips*

Left: A two-car Cravens DMU waits in the hope of passengers at Sudbury prior to making the return journey to Colchester in September 1973. In the years after closure was refused the condition of the unstaffed station deteriorated considerably, broken windows, peeling paint, weeds, rust-covered rails and the abandoned northbound platform all combining to create a depressing scene. This was the second Sudbury station and opened on 9 August 1865 with the extension to Haverhill, the original station becoming the town's goods depot. In this view signalling appears to remain, although the signalman's job can hardly have been the most exacting! In order to allow extension of a leisure centre the station was replaced in October 1991 by a new one immediately to the east, but the footbridge behind the train survives, having been relocated to Chappel & Wakes Colne. Freight services were withdrawn south of Sudbury in December 1964, but (at the time of writing, at least) passenger facilities seem to be assured. *David Mitchell*

A sunny winter's day, 14 January 1967, at Long Melford, between Sudbury and Haverhill, with a Derby Lightweight two-car set forming the 13.44 Cambridge–Sudbury service. The thinly populated central area of East Anglia has seen extensive line and station closures, and Long Melford fared no better than many other towns and villages: the line from here to Bury St Edmunds closed to passengers in April 1961, some freight surviving until 1965. The Sudbury–Shelford line lasted a little longer, freight services ceasing on 31 October 1966. The passenger service was due to be withdrawn north of Sudbury on 31 December of the same year, but there was a delay whilst various local authorities considered subsidising the line. In the event the cost of track renewal was such that no financial assistance was forthcoming, and the line duly closed on 6 March 1967. *Roy Patterson*

Left: The problems faced by the railways in rural East Anglia in the motor age are epitomised in this scene recorded on 15 August 1964. Apart from the railway itself, the only economic activity appears to be agriculture, and there is clearly only the most scattered population. Trying to eke out a living in such inauspicious surroundings, a two-car Derby Lightweight DMU is seen heading away from the camera near Stoke on a Colchester–Cambridge working. The lighter-coloured panel between the cab door and the windows of the passenger accommodation was to protect the paintwork from damage during the exchange of single-line tablets. Whilst the earliest Derby Lightweight cars were given the 'red triangle' coupling code, most had the 'yellow diamond' control system, the symbols being clearly visible on the end of the vehicle. This system predated the standard 'blue square' arrangement, but it was not considered economical to modify the controls on these cars to enable them to work in multiple with 'blue square' units.
John Beckett

Right: A two-car Cravens DMU leaves Saffron Walden on 14 July 1963 with an afternoon train to Audley End. On these cars the aluminium windscreen frames were generally left unpainted, but this attractive feature was lost when the drab corporate livery of overall blue was applied. The leading vehicle sports the yellow panel which replaced the warning 'whiskers' and is also fitted with the two-character headcode panel as carried by later-built cars of this type. The standard Cravens units such as that pictured became Class 105 under the TOPS scheme. Saffron Walden was linked to the main Cambridge line at Audley End from 23 November 1865, an extension to the Colchester–Cambridge line opening in October the following year. As was the case with many lines in East Anglia, World War 2 brought heavier traffic, in this instance petroleum. The line was 'dieselised' in 1958, initially using four-wheeled railbuses, but despite carrying some London commuter traffic it closed to passengers on 7 September 1964 and to all traffic in December of the same year.
John Beckett

Left: The Midland & Great Northern Joint Railway (M&GNJR) linked Peterborough and Little Bytham with Norwich, Yarmouth and Cromer. Passenger services on the line were largely withdrawn from 2 March 1959, but various parts of the system continued to enjoy freight facilities for some years thereafter. In this view, recorded on 27 May 1961, a goods train heads north through Whitwell & Reepham, between Norwich City and Melton Constable, hauled by British Thomson-Houston Type 1 Bo-Bo No D8206. Having entered traffic on 19 May 1958, the locomotive would see only 10 years' service, saw on 30 September 1968. As the class was not particularly successful the last members were taken out of traffic in 1971, although four locomotives served for a further 10 years or so as stationary carriage-heating units. Unusually for a diesel, No D8206 would be cut up at Dai Woodham's scrapyard at Barry, South Wales, in February 1970. *Colour-Rail*

Left: Although nearly all passenger services on the erstwhile M&GNJR were withdrawn on 2 March 1959 the section between Melton Constable and Cromer remained open, the former — once a railway crossroads — becoming the terminus (for passenger trains) of a circuitous branch line for Norwich via Sheringham. Seen awaiting departure from Melton Constable for Norwich Thorpe on 20 September 1962 is a lightweight Metropolitan-Cammell DMU comprising two cars from the first batch (of 58). These units were equipped with the 'yellow diamond' control system (note the jumper sockets below the windscreen) and were thus compatible with the Derby Lightweights. Metropolitan-Cammell supplied a total of 760 diesel cars to British Railways, but this series, completed in 1956, survived only until 1969. Although externally similar to Class 101 they were of a different specification and did not receive a TOPS class number. *Colour-Rail*

On Saturday 19 September 1964 a Derby Lightweight DMU stands at Mundesley-on-Sea, having arrived probably from Norwich Thorpe. The oil tail lamp is still on the rear lamp-iron, and a boy is looking through the open cab door. Mundesley-on-Sea station was on the Norfolk & Suffolk Joint Committee line, which ran from North Walsham to Cromer. This was formerly owned by the Great Eastern and the M&GNJR and was opened in mid-1898. It was extended to Cromer in 1906 as part of a drive to open up the north-east Norfolk coast, but this enterprise failed, and the line beyond Mundesley closed in April 1953. By the time of the photograph the once-splendid station building was in decay but nevertheless shows how high aspirations had been. The track layout suggests that the remaining traffic has been concentrated on the main platform. Three Gresley-designed vehicles, seeing out their days as camping coaches, are using some of the spare platform capacity, and perhaps the group walking along the island platform has just arrived for a holiday in one of them. The introduction of DMUs failed to save the Mundesley-on-Sea branch, and passenger services would be withdrawn on 5 October 1964, closure to all traffic following on 28 December. *Roy Patterson*

Left: On a glorious 25 July 1964 a two-car Derby Lightweight unit leaves the down platform at North Walsham Main on what may be a shunting move following an arrival from Norwich Thorpe. Of particular interest is the signal behind the train, the smaller arm on the right presumably controlling access to what appears to be a loop on the up side. North Walsham Main, on the former Great Eastern (GE) line from Norwich to Cromer, is still open at the time of writing. However, it lost its rather grand suffix some years after closure of the adjacent North Walsham Town station, which was on the former M&GNJR line from Melton Constable to Yarmouth (Beach). The railway network in Norfolk has contracted very significantly, particularly since the 1950s, and as a result North Walsham has since 1964 been no more than a wayside station on a branch from Norwich to Sheringham. However, the line is of some interest as, *en route* to Cromer, it includes the last remaining section of the Norfolk & Suffolk Joint Committee line and similarly, onwards to Sheringham, covers the only part of the M&GN still in everyday use. *Neil Davenport*

Below left: Another photograph taken at North Walsham Main on the same day shows Brush Type 2 A1A-A1A No D5568 arriving with an unidentified southbound train. The first coach is a Gresley-designed vehicle. The train is possibly a through express to London or the Midlands, although by 1964, when this photograph was taken, regular services would have been confined to summer Saturdays. The Norwich–Sheringham line saw a marked reduction in fortunes during the 1950s and '60s, year-round daily through

services disappearing in 1962, the last to survive being the 'Broadsman'. By the early 1970s the only seasonal train remaining was a Summer Saturday Liverpool Street service formed of DMU stock. In January 1967 the local services became conductor-guard-operated, and in 1968 the line survived a closure proposal. Since then, however, the picture has brightened with considerable population growth: North Walsham, for example, expanded from 5,014 in 1961 to 11,998 in 2001. At the time of writing there is an hourly weekday service. *Neil Davenport*

Below: Having arrived from King's Lynn, a Cravens-built two-car DMU stands at Hunstanton, on Saturday 15 February 1969, less than three months before closure (on 5 May). The sea is visible behind the railway, and this had brought much holiday and excursion traffic to the line since it was opened from King's Lynn on 3 October 1862. However, the sparse winter traffic meant that the line faced a bleak future once the motor age dawned. Through trains, including the 'Fenman', had all disappeared by 1967, and only local services remained; these had been provided by DMUs since November 1958. Other economies made in later years included the abolition of station staff and the replacement of traditional level crossings with automatic barriers. The snow in the foreground of the picture emphasises the simplification of the track layout, which resulted in the retention of only the single platform occupied by the train. Sadly, despite all these efforts, the economics of the line were such that closure was inevitable. *John Hayward*

It is well known that the development of the motor vehicle caused many stations and lines to close, service withdrawals starting in earnest in the 1930s. However, it was passenger traffic that was hit first, and in many instances goods lasted until well after World War 2. Typical of a branch with a lengthy goods-only existence was that to Hadleigh, which left the Great Eastern main line at Bentley, between Manningtree and Ipswich. Passenger traffic ceased as early as February 1932, but the line, opened in 1847, continued to see freight trains until 19 April 1965. The branch served an important agricultural area and still seems prosperous in this photograph, taken on 20 April 1962, of Brush Type 2 No D5544 preparing to leave Hadleigh for the run back to the junction. The train appears to have a number of brake vans attached for the use of the enthusiasts seen on the left; such trips, enabling a journey along a closed section of line, were once quite commonplace, but the elimination of the brake van from general use ensured their demise. The redundant shunt signals and cabinets in front of the mineral wagons to the right of the picture are, perhaps, symptomatic of a decline that would ultimately prove terminal. *Colour-Rail*

Right: Opened in 1867 from Mellis (between Stowmarket and Diss on the Great Eastern main line to Norwich), the three-mile branch to Eye lost its passenger trains as early as 2 February 1931 but, like the Hadleigh branch, retained freight facilities for many years afterwards. North British Type 2 Bo-Bo No D6129 shunts wooden-bodied open wagons at the branch terminus on 27 May 1960. The Eye branch closed completely on 13 July 1964. *Colour-Rail*

Below right: BR/Sulzer 1,160hp Type 2 Bo-Bo No D5041 awaits departure from Framlingham with a short goods train in April 1965. This type is not generally associated with East Anglia, but a number found work there in their early days, No D5041 being allocated for some years to Ipswich depot. This locomotive shows some of the early features of Modernisation Plan diesels, including the access doors cut into the front end and the disc headcode display. The 'blue star' coupling code can be clearly seen above the buffer beam. As was the case with DMUs, only locomotives bearing the same code could be worked in multiple, the 'blue star' code applying at this time to all diesel-electric locomotives fitted with electro-pneumatic control. Under the TOPS scheme No D5041 would become Class 24 No 24 041, remaining in service thus until July 1976, although not being cut up (at BREL Swindon) until June 1978. The Framlingham branch, opened from Wickham Market (on the Ipswich–Lowestoft line) in 1859, had lost its passenger service in November 1952, but freight services survived for some years afterwards, being withdrawn on 19 April 1965, the same date as those to Hadleigh. *Colour-Rail*

Left: A four-car DMU formation *en route* from Ipswich to Lowestoft leaves the staggered platforms at Saxmundham, on the East Suffolk line, in August 1972. The train consists of two twin units, that nearer the camera having been built by the Gloucester Railway Carriage & Wagon Co Ltd; the leading carriage, DMBS No E51111, had entered service in November 1957 and would be a relatively early casualty, being withdrawn in September 1973. The second set is of mixed formation, the leading vehicle (the third coach of the train) being a Metropolitan-Cammell car, whilst the rearmost is a Cravens. These types became Classes 100, 101 and 105 respectively under TOPS. Class 101 would be the last of the Modernisation Plan DMU designs to operate in significant numbers, still being employed on some Manchester Piccadilly suburban services as late as December 2003. The East Suffolk line, happily, continues to operate, although survival has not been easy. The direct route from Beccles to Yarmouth via Haddiscoe was lost in 1959, and, of the branches, only those to Felixstowe and the freight spur serving the power station at Sizewell survive. Closure of the East Suffolk line, proposed in 1965, was refused, but the intermediate stations were unstaffed from 1967, and the line was partially singled in 1984. *Colour-Rail*

Below: A two-car Derby Lightweight DMU stands at the branch terminus at Aldeburgh prior to departure for Ipswich in May 1966. Traffic appears to be significant — somewhat surprisingly, as passenger services would be withdrawn on 12 September of that year. The station originally had an overall roof, but this had already been removed by the date of the photograph. The line from Saxmundham, between Ipswich and Lowestoft, was completed as far as Leiston in 1859, the extension to Aldeburgh being opened on 12 April 1860. The branch fostered little economic development in the area and led a quiet existence, DMUs being introduced in June 1956. Aldeburgh lost its goods facilities on 30 November 1959, but construction of the power station at Sizewell prolonged the passenger service and, after the latter's withdrawal, ensured retention of part of the branch for freight traffic, although the section of line beyond the power station — to the terminus at Aldeburgh — was closed completely. *Colour-Rail*

Above: Photographed after a sudden downpour on 26 July 1966, a three-car Derby suburban set awaits departure from North Woolwich as the 16.30 to Cheshunt. Twenty such units were built for the Lea Valley line in north-east London, being fitted with 238hp Rolls-Royce engines to give better acceleration. They also had hydraulic (as against the standard mechanical) transmission. As the control system was pneumatic, rather than the electro-pneumatic system used in 'blue square' units, these cars were given the unique 'orange star' coupling code, and the symbol is clearly visible on the front of the unit in the photograph. Bodywork was unusual for DMUs on the Eastern Region, featuring a slam door to each seating bay. Displaced from the Great Eastern lines by electrification, in 1969, the units, by now TOPS Class 125, moved to the ex-Great Northern line, but all would be withdrawn by early 1977. At the time of writing the line to North Woolwich, opened on 14 June 1847, is the latest to close on the national rail network, passenger services having being withdrawn on 10 December 2006 upon the opening of the Docklands Light Railway extension to the nearby King George V station. The station building seen behind the train has since 1984 been used as a railway museum, and it is envisaged that this will be further developed in concert with the establishment of a rail training facility using the closed line to Custom House. *Terry Phillips*

Back cover: Brush Type 2 A1A-A1A No 5636 arrives at Audley End with the 17.36 Liverpool Street–Cambridge on 15 July 1972. This very successful class of locomotive, built between 1957 and 1962, has been associated with the Eastern Region throughout its life. Under the TOPS computerised numbering scheme this example became Class 31/1 No 31 212, in which guise it was to remain in service until December 1991. *Terry Phillips*